Memoirs of an Alias

Memoirs of an Alias

Jason Heroux

Mansfield Press

Printed in Canada

Library and Archives Canada Cataloguing in Publication

Heroux, Jason, 1971 –
Memoirs of an alias / Jason Heroux.

Poems.
ISBN 1-894469-18-6

I. Title.

PS8565.E825M45 2004 C811'.54 C2004-905372-8

Design: Marijke Friesen
Cover Photo: Stuart Macmillan

The publication of *Memoirs of an Alias* has been generously supported by The Canada Council for the Arts and The Ontario Arts Council.

The Canada Council for the Arts since 1957 | Le Conseil des Arts du Canada depuis 1957

Ontario Arts Council
Conseil des Arts de l'Ontario

Mansfield Press Inc.
25 Mansfield Avenue, Toronto, Ontario, Canada. M6J 2A9
Publisher: Denis De Klerck
www.mansfieldpress.net

For Soheir

and in memory of Jeff Carter

(1970 – 1999)

CONTENTS

STORY

One summer night a stranger
threw an artificial leg onto my lawn,

made of plastic, leather, steel.
The garbagemen left it there.

Sunday, my neighbour put on
a yard sale. He rang my bell

and swore, "Christ, you got to get
rid of that thing because people

think I'm trying to sell it. I'm
losing business." All our yards

are jammed together – my other
neighbour grows a garden in hers

and throws a tattered trenchcoat
and fedora over the For Sale sign

in my yard, to frighten off birds.
I haven't received mail in weeks.

Last night, I carried the leg to
the lake and threw it into the dark

blue sheets of water where it thrashed
as if waking from a terrible dream.

EVENING POSTSCRIPT

The taxi rumbles
        in the empty street
like a straw at the bottom
        of a glass.
A moment later
        everything is quiet:

the dead have called
        us here to make
an important announcement,
        and all
the grass leans
        in one direction like
microphones during
        a press conference.

The stores are closed,
        but the earth is open.
Our shadows pass through
        the grassy turnstiles,

and the spider in her web
        wakes up twitching
like a small dark glove
        when the hand enters.

THE PIZZA DELIVERYMAN

The pizza deliveryman has my address, like an angel of death, and he is driving through this cold night to reach me. It's too late for him to turn back now. It's too late for everything to be the way it was before. How much time do I have? He knows this city like the back of his hand, and his car has a tank full of gas. Even if I jumped on a train and left town before he arrived, I'd always smell the aroma of hot, steaming pizza behind me. Even if I started a new life in some other city, the doorbell would ring one night, and I'd see his car outside, with no one in it, the engine running. Lord, give me the strength to accept the things I cannot change. When the time comes, give me the strength to open the door.

THE FLEA MARKET A FEW MINUTES BEFORE CLOSING

The clocks on the table are all stopped. Their hands reaching toward us, the arms of beggar children in a crowded city square; they need time and I have none to spare. Next to them a table of old telephones, with people's voices still lingering somewhere in the wires, miners trapped in collapsed tunnels. The evening light shines filtered through a dusty window and hovers in air, stuck in place like a rusted bolt. Standing in the flea market a few minutes before closing I heard someone whisper the secret of happiness on earth: *never look forward to anything, and don't ever look back.*

EDWARD HOPPER'S *East Side Interior*

Sleepy woman, staring out the window,
I've been thinking of you a lot lately.
The black sewing machine on the table
in front of you stitches the pale fabric
like a dark hen pecking at scattered food.
I can tell you didn't sleep well last night.
You are sewing curtains for the window,

staring outside, with a tired look on your
face and a crooked picture frame hanging
on the sunlit wall right behind your head.
I've often wondered what you're gazing at.
Your blouse still slightly unbuttoned after
breast-feeding the baby asleep in the stroller;
the light growing heavier on your shoulders.

DARK JARS

There is a place
where doctors
remove people's shadows
from their bodies for free.

A friend of mine went there.

I never saw him again.

But he told me about it
last night in a dream.

"The shadows are kept
in jars," he said.

"The jars are so dark.
They all look the same.
And no one knows whose
is whose."

NOON

Under an entranced sun: the clock's scissors shut
for a minute; the truth belongs to a small yellow
ball lying in grass.

A few construction workers sit under a tree
eating lunch as the wind gathers twigs and ribbons
for its nest in the next world.

There is one rain puddle left in the street:
an upside down bell whose silence is heard
all over the world.

The old and young alike walk the short planks
of their own shadows and the truth is: the small
yellow ball may never be picked
up again.

SUMMER

I open the window, an empty drawer
in the sky's invisible dresser, and hear
people's voices, conversational scraps

ripped in half like old lottery tickets,
and traffic on a distant road rumbling
softly as spit in a trumpet's bowels.

It is somehow summer again,
and the clock on the kitchen wall ticks
with nonchalance, a bored secretary

filing her fingernails; and the birds
outside, not quite singing, resemble
little smoke detectors beeping

to let us know their batteries have
been dying for centuries. The past
is calling, but today doesn't answer.

The moment sits slightly askew
on its shadow. Like a telephone
that hasn't been hung up properly.

PAGE FROM A DREAMBOOK

I saw a friend of mine,
who had been dead
a long time,
in a park counting
something and I asked
what he was counting.
"Numbers," he said,
looking at me,
in a panic.
I started to get scared
too. Then an old woman
walked through the park
feeding the statues.
"I hear their stomachs
grumbling," she said
to us, balancing
small white crumbs
between their lips.

LIFE IN A NOVEL

The trouble started when the light bulbs began to burn out in the novel. The author never replaced them. We realized we were on our own and could do whatever we wanted. I was originally just another nobody in an overcrowded paragraph: a stranger with "a distant look on his face" carrying "a black umbrella" who passes the happy couple in the street. Now I'm the only character left. Digging graves in the cold hard ground with my umbrella. I'm afraid the next person who takes this novel from the shelf will die of shock after seeing what we've done to ourselves.

THE SPOON

He picked up the spoon.
"What are you doing?" the spoon asked.
"I'm about to eat lunch," he said.

"But I'll drown if you put me into the soup."
"You won't drown," he said. "You're a spoon."
"I'll drown," the spoon said.

He put the spoon in the soup and held it there for a long time. The handle twitched. Little bubbles appeared on the surface of the soup. He was afraid to lift the spoon up, afraid to put it inside his mouth.

The soup grew colder and colder.

SOLITUDE

One
in the morning,
                    a vacant
street, the birds listening.
Streetlamps weeping slowly falling snow.

                                        I look back
and see my footprints . . . empty
teacups left on a long white tablecloth.

No one knows where I am except a blind
wind passing its hands over my face.

FEAR DIARY

Morning, some smoke rises from a chimney
like a clump of grey hair pulled from a drain.
Young nervous men knock on my door and ask
    if I believe in God.

Coffee trembles in its cup as transport
trucks pass the house. I'm afraid of the grass.
The way it twitches in wind like the tails
    of mice caught in traps.

NOVEMBER EVENING

Darkness enters the window
like a bruise
under a fingernail.
In the middle of the road
a stone's shadow is waiting
to be let back into the stone.

Sometimes someone in the crowd
stops, turns around, and walks back
because they have just remembered
or forgotten something important.

One by one leaves fall and stick
like postage stamps to the ground
as if the world was being sent
somewhere far away.

HELL

Hell is crowded, but you don't notice at first. You're sitting down, and you realize your chair is a person, on their hands and knees, wobbling under your weight. You knock on a door, but it's not a door, it's a person, and you've punched them in the chest.

BRIEF CASE

One morning a man, walking to work, drops his briefcase open on a sidewalk and notices the mess it makes. He spends the rest of the day falling in love with the spilled material from his brief case. He decides to leave his wife and family.

Not wanting to pick the material off the ground, the man builds a small house on the sidewalk for the two of them. In the privacy of his own home, he impregnates the spilled material from his brief case.

His friends think it has gone too far. They say . . . they don't know what to say. They think he should keep the spilled material from his brief case as a mistress, nothing more.

"My friends think I should leave you," the man says to the spilled material from his brief case one morning in bed. "What do you think? Do you love me?"

There is no answer. The spilled material from his brief case can't talk, but if it could, it would say, "I'm late for work."

The man thinks the spilled material from his brief case is keeping something from him. It never says a word to him and he doesn't know how to take the silence.

I am late for work, I am late for work, the spilled material from his brief case thinks to itself, whenever the topic turns to love.

THE STONE-EATERS

Things were so bad we ate rocks to keep alive, little bland stones that cracked our teeth, because that was all there was to eat. Whenever we found a few stones we'd kill one by beating it to death with the other. But when the stones realized we were eating them they started to hide by lying very still, and it was difficult to spot them because they blended in so well with the terrain. Then things got worse. Now, if we're lucky enough to find a stone, we suck on it, slowly, and hope it'll last us the rest of our lives.

A MOMENT'S NOTICE

A small dead spider on a grey parking meter with its time expired.

"THE STARS HAVE GROWN . . ."

The stars have grown
stale, hardened, like gum
stuck under
the sky's dark
school desk.

The only way
to write about the dead
is to use a pen without ink

and in the silence
you hear your own heart

pecking at nothing, as if
it was food

while the clock hands move through
the day like cutlery through a meal.

"TODAY I'M MORE ALIVE THAN USUAL . . ."

Today I'm more alive than usual.
I am still Jason Heroux but I'm also
the little doorstep everyone walks over,
and the forgotten ladder left leaning

against a wall on Sunday, and a cigarette butt
on the cold sidewalk waiting to be swept up,
because today I'm less dead than I usually am.

Everyone remembers the crime of when
I walked through an old cobweb.
And the little stone I kicked, once.

So you must be Jason Heroux, they say.
Yes, I'm Jason Heroux, but I'm also
the snowflake falling through the air,
and the next one, and the one after that,

but not the fourth one, or the fifth,
no, just the first three, and then that's it.

WAR AGAINST THE BABIES

They appeared out of nowhere, going through our garbage bags at night and leaving behind their droppings in our cupboards.

We made the mistake of being nice to the babies in the beginning, giving them food, shelter, and medical attention.

Then more of them came.

The filthy babies took our land and suckled the breasts of our wives as if they were whores.

It was our land. They took it.

We had no choice but to wage war against those damn babies.

They were easy to kill, thank God,
but there are still so many of them left to kill.
And we're starting to get tired of killing them.

The heartless babies know they're wearing us down.

And to top it all off, they're slowly beginning to resemble us . . . . One day soon we'll have to wage war against ourselves, and lose, in order to defeat the bloodthirsty babies.

NIGHT WINDOWS

At night
windows
wear
mourning
for
their own
lost lives.

MAUPASSANT

A few years
after he coaxed
his insane brother
into an asylum cell
by showing him the view
from its window
Maupassant
went insane himself.
One night he raised
a pistol to his head
and pulled the trigger,
then pulled it again –
someone had hid his bullets.
He turned his room upside down,
found a letter
opener, and stabbed it
several times into his throat.
He woke up the next day
in a hospital
and wanted to enlist
in the war even though
there was no war.
His doctors decided
to show Maupassant
his boat – Bel
Ami II – docked
in a harbour at Cannes,
hoping the sight of it
would startle him sane.
Did the trick work?
He took one look
at his yacht and cried.

THE BATH

Sentenced to death by Nero
Seneca asked a doctor
to slit
the veins in his arms
and thighs – his blood
drained so slow
he also
demanded a draught of poison,
but his veins were
slit
so the poison never reached
his heart. He wouldn't die,
what could they do?

They drew a bath,
a real bath, the kind
we take when we have
an hour to ourselves and
the water cools as if to say

you can't stay here forever

which is probably what it said
to Seneca as he sprinkled
the bloody bathwater
over his head and dedicated it
to Jupiter the Deliverer
just as sunlight
razored
through the thick steam.

HAYDN, BACH AND MOZART

Haydn

One day Haydn was asked to be the drummer in a parade on the streets of Hainburg. Franz Joseph was so young he could not carry a drum so it was strapped to a hunchbacked boy in front of him. He fell in love with the daughter of a wigmaker, but she refused him. Out of spite he married her ugly, older sister. On May 10, 1809, Napoleon invaded Vienna, and a large cannonball fell near Haydn's house. He died of complications.

Bach

Johann Sebastian abandoned his position of organist at the church of Anstadt in order to better himself and, in fact, his next job paid eighty-five gulden, twelve bushels of corn, six trusses of brushwood, free moving expenses, and three pounds of fish every year as a bonus. He had two families, twenty children, a lot of mouths to feed, and they all talked at once. He wrote two hundred organ compositions, cantatas, and concertos, and when he died the written music was left in the cupboards of the St. John's vestry and was used by pupils wishing to wrap their sandwiches.

Mozart

In Mannheim, Mozart gave lessons to Aloysia Weber and could not get her out of his thoughts: he kept imagining her breasts filling like a pool of rain in his palms, her vagina poised like a bat between arches. Then he met her sister Konstanze and the same thing happened. He married Konstanze, danced in his room to keep warm while writing "Don Giovanni" and pawned his silverware to ride trains with royalty. When Wolfgang's wife became ill he began walking around the room with a finger pressed to his lips to remind him not to make noise.

IN FEBRUARY

In February the stones in the road are sluggish and slow
as if they ate a large heavy meal right before entering the world.
Snow-covered tree branches resemble tangled silver necklaces
                    left too long in a jewelery box.

I wake with my pulse throbbing impatiently against my skin,
and I'm suddenly so alive my body feels a size too small.
A little after dawn streetlamps switch off, a search party
                    finding what was lost.

DUSK

Distant birdsongs clatter together:
        unused cutlery cleared from a table.
The sunlit window of an empty house
        turns yellow as the leaf of a dying plant.
Evening light shuffles the tangled shadows

        of tree limbs across the brick wall.
The newspaper page lying on the ground
        is an old rug world events are swept under.
Cars buzz through dusk's haze, frantic bees
        searching for a way out of the smoke-filled hive.

This evening the mountains are covered with fog
        and seem off in their own little corners,
guests at a party who don't know anyone;
        and rain puddles in the street grow dark
as photographs taken with the lens cap still on.

UNFURNISHED APARTMENT

All the curtains
are gone: moonlight
drifts across the floor

like a loose band-aid.
The corners of rooms
are angels with walls

for wings, wearing halos
made by spiders.
There are empty clothes

hangers hanging in the closet
bobbing gently in place
like ducks sleeping on water.

SPRING, AT THE CORNER OF MONTREAL AND QUEEN

It is not spring
until
the amazing
prostitutes emerge
until the woman with
the purple jaguar
tattoo
crouched
on the trunk
of one breast
asks for a cigarette.
Where is
the woman with
the caved-in face
who stumbled
in heels
like a newborn fawn
over uneven roads?
I miss
how her purse
swung like a monkey
from her small
bruised shoulders
and how
she waited in
the warm rain
that stood up like hair
on the back of my neck.

MIDNIGHT IN A ROOM

A dark light bulb dangles
        from the ceiling like a rotten tooth
and a foul-mouthed cockroach
is running around spreading
        lies about me, saying
I tried to slaughter him
with my ex-wife's slipper.
        But he's not telling
the whole story.
Outside, raindrops
        the size of rats
abandon a cloud's sinking ship.

THE NEWSPAPER

Incurable diseases. Famine. War.
Yet the newspaper seems so delicate –
rolled up and wrapped in
plastic to protect it from the weather.

"ON RAINY DAYS . . ."

On rainy days
the early mornings
resemble evenings

and the middle-aged
insect on the ceiling no longer
knows what to do with its life.

A large dark crow stumbles
uncomfortably across the street
like a right shoe on the left foot.

Everything is a little confused except
for the clear-headed raindrops rushing
full speed into this one-and-only world.

HAIKU

All the stores are closed

the sun shines into a mannequin's
half-opened eyes

a crowd of faces –

who can identify
the back of their own head?

the old grey fence in rain –
half-standing, half-fallen

where we all walk through

HERE SOMEWHERE

There is a real world here somewhere, mixed in with the unreal one.
In the unreal world stones don't say much, but in the real world
they talk your ear off; when the heavy trucks drive by
the little stones in the road quiver like voice-boxes singing opera.
There is a real death here somewhere, mixed in with the unreal one.
The unreal death lasts forever but real death is just a little nap.
A telephone ringing somewhere in the universe will wake you up.
There is a real day here somewhere, mixed in with the unreal one.
We don't have much time. Ring the earth's doorbell, but don't run
away at the last moment. Unreal days never end,
but each real day is only a couple of minutes long.

FINAL EXAM

I have a pencil
that's so old
and weak I have
to hold it with
both hands to help
it across the page.
"Oh God . . . oh God,"
it writes, leaving
the answers blank.

HUNGER

Hands.
They have grown around the heart,
knuckling like a rib cage,
reaching.

Hours, hours
imagining the pick-up truck
stacked with corn.
We hear bats clapping

through damp air, voices
broken by a hair
in the throat.

The bell rings.
In the sink
our hands jump, whip

like salmon sheathed in stream.

ATLANTIC LETTERS

for Darryl Whetter

It is early in the morning;
the sky has not yet arrived.
The truth could be that our blood,
reeled through us like film,
needs another person's darkness
to develop in.

RESTAURANT, 4 A.M.

The man
near the window
is smiling
at me, crushing his cigarette
into the center
of his plate.

And there is a woman
by the door, who is
smiling as she hitches
her stocking
an extra inch
above the thigh.

I smile at both of them,
just in case
we all happen to know
each other.

WINTER IMAGES

The sky draws
its curtains
shut to wander

nude in its room.

A joyous snowfall
hops around
on a hundred legs.

Our street is still

in bed with white
sheets pulled
up to its chin.

THE TALE OF AN EXTRAORDINARY DAY

I woke,
all of a sudden, up
from a nap
unable
to believe it at first.

When it falls
the leaf
goes
everywhere
without itself.

The phone rang,
I picked it up, saying:
hello? A man asked
if I was who
I was.

Looking twice
at the clock I saw
the same
time
both times

and heard,
of all things,
a person's key
in the hallway unlocking
a person's door.

LETTER TO A FRIEND IN THE NEXT WORLD

The early morning
dust particles leap
sunbeams like fleas
on a dog. Outside,
traffic flows up
a one-way street.
Letters sent, return,
unopened. Your name,
your street number,
crossed out in black ink:
unused railway tracks
overgrown with weeds.
A bright day, your shadow
has disappeared from earth:
a dark parachute opening
when you were born;
it's been packed again
ready for your next jump.

BEGINNING OF AUTUMN

The morning sun
behind the clouds:
weak as a heartbeat
under a suit of armor.

Grey light swept up
into the window's dustpan.

At the beginning of every autumn
I start noticing more and more stones
in the road: little stones stuffed
with stoniness, ready to burst;

little stones with their strange shapes,
like half-melted candies
spit from a mouth;

little stones the colour
of fogged-up eyeglasses.

At the beginning of every autumn
I see people walking slowly across
the street like they've arrived
somewhere too early,

as if they live their whole lives
waiting for a store inside them
to open its doors.

At the beginning of every autumn
the leaves start to resemble
the old, withered receipts

of things we purchased
long ago in our dreams.

ON THE CORNER

A red traffic light
paralyzes its prey
with a silent
thirty-second roar
as delinquent sunlit
trees spray paint
shadow graffiti
on the walls.

The man sweeping
the sidewalk
moves through
the crowd with his head
bowed, eyes lowered.
His stainless steel
watchband glitters
in the setting sun.

I pass a café closing
up for the evening
and see two green
patio chairs
stacked over
each other:
long-legged insects
making love.

Pale smoke rises
from a chimney,
a cast around
the air's broken arm.
The dead take their world
with them; at night I hear
their faded footsteps stamp
the sidewalk's passport.

AFTER THE STORM

The clouds open
and the old snow by the side of the road
        glitters
with the intensity of tinfoil in a microwave.

The last few drops of rain tap a telegraphed
        message
of transparent morse code against the window.

Birds balanced on the tips of branches squeak
        like erasers
at the end of pencils:
the world is writing its entrance exam.

There is one person on the street.
Think of all the people who were needed to make
        this one person.
She stands still,
        in a daze,
like a number after a long, baffling math equation.

OCTOBER RAINFALL

When it rains in October
our private thoughts
feel a little exposed,

as if wandering around
in our heads
wearing hospital gowns.

A raindrop's wrecking ball
demolishes the puddle's
rooftop,

for a moment
the world
is temporarily closed
like the ears of someone
swimming underwater

and our souls are the colour
of dark wet stones that glisten
like olive pits spit from a mouth.

LIGHT SWITCH

You are the blind
wall's white
walking
cane.

Too short
to reach
the floor,

you dangle

in mid-air.
It's not
your fault

the ground is so far away.

PRINCE GEORGE, BRITISH COLUMBIA

Visiting Prince George, British Columbia,
we drove by the emptiest-looking cemetery
I had ever seen. People must spend
their whole lives trying not to die in that town.

There was one particular tombstone
covered with fresh flowers, surrounded
by footprints in the snow: the grave
of a nineteen-year-old summer student

who died in an accident at the sawmill.
Her sudden violent death made everyone
in town shudder the way walls shudder
when a door is slammed shut too quickly.

The many footprints in the snow-covered
graveyard resembled air-holes to help
the dead continue breathing, like a firefly
caught for a little while in the earth's jar.

HAPPINESS

The early morning light has a trace of yesterday left in it, and spiders feel the long night's work aching in their legs. Classical music on the radio tracks Eighteenth century mud through the house. It's okay to cry quietly to yourself for no reason. It's okay to feel alive for only ten minutes a day. The ticking clock shivers, as if holding back little sneezes so as not to wake us. Sometimes when you think the street is empty you suddenly see another person two blocks away, and feel right next to them. Sometimes a small bicycle leans against the candy store window like a bee hovering in front of a half-opened flower.

ACKNOWLEDGEMENTS

Grateful acknowledgement is made to the following publications, in which a number of these poems previously appeared: The Adirondack Review, Another Toronto Quarterly, The Antigonish Review, Arc, Axe Factory Review, Breathing Fire 2 (Harbour Publishing), Burning Ambitions (Rush Hour Revisions), The Brobdingnagian Times, Can We Have Our Ball Back, Cenotaph Pocket Edition, Chance Magazine, Crimson Feet, Existere, The Fiddlehead, Ink, Jones Av., The Journal Of Contemporary Anglo-Scandinavian Poetry, The Lilliput Review, Microbe Revue, Modern Haiku, The Nashwaak Review, The Pedestal Magazine, The Phone Book, Presence, Qwerty, Regina Weese, Sidereality Magazine, Siren, Sub-terrain, Tickle Ace, Urban Graffiti, Wascana Review, and Windsor Review.

Several of these poems also appeared in two chapbooks: *The Days Are Hardly Here At All* (Microbe Editions, Belgium) and *Leaving The Road* (Mercutio Press, Montreal).

Miron Białoszewski's "A Ballad of Going Down to a Store" inspired "The Tale Of An Extraordinary Day." And Larry Levis' "The Crimes of the Shade Trees" inspired "Today I'm More Alive Than Usual…"

The poetry of Jason Heroux has appeared in literary journals in Canada, the US, Belgium, England, Ireland and India. He was born in Montreal and now lives and writes in Kingston, Ontario. *Memoirs of an Alias* is his first book.